Picture credits:
l: Left, r: Right, t: Top, b: Bottom, c: Centre

6tl: FRANKA BRUNS/ ASSOCIATED PRESS, 7r: AL BEHRMAN/ ASSOCIATED PRESS, 8tl: THOMAS KIENZLE/ ASSOCIATED PRESS, 8b: DIEGO GIUDICE/ ASSOCIATED PRESS, 9: DIMITRI MESSINIS/ ASSOCIATED PRESS, 10tr: RANDY BROOKS/ ASSOCIATED PRESS, 10b: Topham / PA, 11: Gautam Singh/ ASSOCIATED PRESS, 12t: CARLO FUMAGALLI/ ASSOCIATED PRESS, 12m: TopFoto / AP, 12b: ProSport / TopFoto, 13: Carlos Alberto Parreira/ ASSOCIATED PRESS, 14b: GENE J. PUSKAR/ ASSOCIATED PRESS, 15: Bill Kostroun/ ASSOCIATED PRESS, 16tl: AL BEHRMAN/ ASSOCIATED PRESS, 16bl: ASSOCIATED PRESS, 17: Getty Images, 18: ALASTAIR GRANT/ ASSOCIATED PRESS, 19t: ROSS SETFORD/ ASSOCIATED PRESS, 19b: ADAM BUTLER/ ASSOCIATED PRESS, 20: Ferrari, 21t: Ferrari, 22tl: ARIEL SCHALIT/ ASSOCIATED PRESS, 22-23b: ADAM NADEL/ ASSOCIATED PRESS, 23tr: RIA Novosti / TopFoto, 25tr: Roger-Viollet / Topfoto, 26l: Professional Sport / TopFoto, 26mr: 2001 Credit:Topham / PA, 27: JOHN GRESS/ ASSOCIATED PRESS, 28tl: TopFoto, 28b: PETER DEJONG/ ASSOCIATED PRESS, 29: PA Photos / Topfoto, 30: PA Photos / Topfoto, 31t: ASSOCIATED PRESS, 31b: ASSOCIATED PRESS, 32: ASSOCIATED PRESS, 33tr: 2000 Credit:Topham Picturepoint, 34tr: ProSport / TopFoto, 34bl: ProSport / TopFoto, 35: Professional Sport / TopFoto, 36: PA Photos / Topfoto, 37tr: TopFoto / UPP, 38tl: opham / ProSport, 38br: Professional Sport / TopFoto, 40: MIRKO GUARRIELLO/ ASSOCIATED PRESS, 41: MASSIMO PINCA/ ASSOCIATED PRESS, 42l: Professional Sport / TopFoto, 42tr: Topham Picturepoint/ ASSOCIATED PRESS, 43: Scott Barbour/Staff/ Gettyimages

Published By Robert Frederick Ltd.
4 North Parade, Bath, BA1 1LF, England

First Published: 2008

# Sporting Records

## CONTENTS

# TRACK ATHLETICS

## FASTEST MARATHON (MEN'S)

Kenyan athlete Wilson Kipsang Kiprotich set a new World Record when he won the Berlin Marathon on September 29, 2013 with his time of 2:03:23, shaving 15 seconds off fellow Kenyan Patrick Makau's record, which he set in the same race in 2011. Kipseng is a two-time winner of the Frankfurt Marathon, and has also won the London Marathon.

## MOST INDIVIDUAL MEDALS AT HALF MARATHON WORLD CHAMPIONSHIPS (WOMEN'S)

Lidia Simon of Romania won a total of eight medals at the Half Marathon World Championships between the years 1996 and 2000. She won three team gold medals, one team silver medal, and one individual bronze medal. The men's record for the half marathon is held by Jifar Tesfaye of Ethiopia.

## 100 M HURDLES (WOMEN'S)

Yordanka Donkova of Bulgaria is a former hurdling athlete who set four World Records in 100 m hurdles, in 1986. Her fifth record of 12.21 seconds remains the Championship Record to this day! In her outstanding career Donkova won an Olympic gold and bronze medal, as well as nine medals at European indoor and outdoor Championships.

## 1000 M (WOMEN'S)

Svetlana Alexandrovna Masterkova, a Russian, is a former middle distance runner who began her professional career as an 800 m runner. Her major breakthrough came in 1991 when she qualified for the World Championships. It was in 1996 that she completed her season by setting two new World Records at two irregular distances — 1000 m and a mile. She set the record over 1000 m on August 23, 1996, in 2:28.98, and the record for the mile on August 14, 1996, in 4:12.56.

## 100 M & 200 M (WOMEN'S)

Florence Griffith-Joyner, popularly known as Flo-Jo, was an American track and field athlete. She still holds the World Record for the 100 m and 200 m. At the 1988 Summer Olympics, she ran the 100 m in 10.49 seconds in the final, beating her nearest rival by three-tenths of a second. In the 200 m quarter-final race she set a new World Record of 21.33 seconds, and won in the final by 0.4 seconds.

### Did You Know?

Athletics is derived from the Greek word 'athlon', meaning 'contest'. It was first included in the modern Olympic Games in 1896. Athletics includes a collection of sports events that involve running, throwing and jumping. They are organised around a 400 m running track. Running events take place on the track while field events take place inside the track.

## FASTEST SPRINTER (MEN'S)

Born on August 21, 1986, Usain Bolt is a Jamaican Sprinter. He currently holds the World Records for the 100m (9.58s) and 200m (19.19s) – the first man to hold both records since full automatic time measurements became mandatory in 1977. He also, along with his teammates, set the World Record for the 4x100m relay with their time of 36.84 seconds.

### LONGEST LONG JUMP (MEN'S)

Michael Anthony Powell, a former American track and field athlete, broke Bob Beamon's 23 year old long jump World Record by 5 cm (2 in), leaping 8.95 m (29.36 ft) at the 1991 World Championships. Powell's accomplishment won him several prestigious awards, including the James E. Sullivan Award and the BBC Sports Personality of the Year Overseas Personality Award in 1991. Powell was the first (and so far the only) person to win the Jack Turnbull Award on four consecutive occasions! This sports star is also the only person to win the Tewaaraton Trophy twice.

### HIGHEST HIGH JUMP (MEN'S)

Javier Sotomayor, a Cuban former athlete and the greatest high jumper of all time, was the first man to clear 2.44 m (8 ft), in July 1989. He also set a World Record with his leap of 2.45 m (8.05 ft) in 1993. Sotomayor began competing at the high jump at the age of 14 and by 1986 he had become the Junior World Champion. Of the 24 all-time best jumps, 17 are Sotomayor's!

### Did You Know?

Historically, poles were used as a practical means of passing over natural obstacles in places such as the marshy provinces of Friesland in the Netherlands.

## POLE VAULT (WOMEN'S)

The World outdoor record in the women's pole vault is held by Yelena Gadzhievna Isinbayeva, a Russian pole-vaulter. In 2009, Isinbayeva set the outdoor World Record at 5.06 m (16.7 ft). In 2012 she also held the World Record for indoor pole vault at 5.01m (16.4 ft). She has set 20 World Records in her career and remains one of the most successful athletes of all time.

## JAVELIN (WOMEN'S)

Czech javelin thrower Barbora Špotáková set the World Record for the longest throw on September 13, 2008 at the World Athletics Final in Stuttgart, Germany. The throw measured 72.28 m (237.1 ft) and surpassed Osleidys Menendez's previous record of 71.7 m (235.2 ft) by 58 cm (1.9 ft).

## DISCUS (MEN'S)

Jürgen Schult, who represented Germany in the discus, set the World Record with a throw of 74.08 m (243 ft). The throw broke the previous record, set by Yuri Dumchev, by a massive 2.22 m (7.28 ft). He represented East Germany in the 1988 Olympics, where he won the gold medal.

## SHOT PUT (MEN'S)

Randy Barnes, an American shot putter, holds the World Record for both indoor and outdoor distance. In 1989, he set a new indoor World Record in Los Angeles with a distance of 22.66 m (74.34 ft). In 1990, he set a new outdoor World Record with a put of 23.12 m (75.85 ft), beating the previous World Record set by Ulf Timmermann.

## POLE VAULT (MEN)

Sergei Bubka, a retired pole vaulter from the Ukraine, is widely considered the greatest pole vaulter ever. He set a World indoor Record of 6.14 m (20.14 ft), in 1994, at Sestriere, having set a World outdoor Record of 6.15 m (20.2 ft) the year before in the Ukraine. Both records remain unbeaten. He has cleared a height of 6 m (19.7 ft) on more than 44 occasions and broken the men's World Record 35 times in his career.

## LARGEST INNINGS IN A TEST MATCH

The West Indian cricketer Brian Lara, popularly known as 'The Prince' in his home country, holds the record for the highest individual innings in Test cricket with an unbeaten 400 runs – set against England in 2004! Lara is widely considered to be one of the greatest batsmen of all time and is the all-time leading run scorer with 11,953. He was also the fastest batsman to 10,000 runs. Lara retired from international cricket in 2007.

## LARGEST ONE DAY INTERNATIONAL INNINGS

India's Virender Sehwag holds the record for the largest innings in a One Day International, scoring 219 runs off 149 balls against the West Indies in 2011. In April 2009, Sehwag became the only Indian to be honoured as the Wisden Leading Cricketer in the World and he is the only player in the world to score a double hundred in ODI and a triple hundred in Test Cricket.

### Did You Know?

Viv Richards is the only person to have played in both World Cup Football and World Cup Cricket! He played for Antigua in World Cup Football and for West Indies in World Cup Cricket.

## BEST BOWLING FIGURES FOR A ONE DAY INTERNATIONAL (ODI)

The record for best ODI bowling figures is held by Chaminda Vaas of Sri Lanka, against Zimbabwe. In this match he took 8 wickets for just 19 runs, in a spell that included a hat-trick of wickets! This successful fast bowler has taken over 350 ODI wickets in his Test match career – one of only three bowlers ever to have done so!

## HIGHEST NUMBER OF TEST SIXES

Australia's Adam Gilchrist has scored more sixes in his test career than any other batsman - 100 to date. He also holds the record for the second fastest ODI century by an Australian. Gilchrist is Australia's most successful wicket keeper and is considered one of the best wicket keeper-batsmen of all time.

## TWENTY20 WORLD CUP FASTEST HALF-CENTURY

Yuvraj Singh of India set a record for the fastest half-century by an individual in the first Twenty20 World Cup, in 2007. He scored his 50 runs in just 12 balls in a match against England, hitting six sixes in one over – a feat that has only been achieved three times previously in top flight cricket, and never previously between two Test nations!

## HIGHEST INDIVIDUAL SCORE IN A WORLD CUP MATCH

Gary Kirsten of South Africa holds the record for the highest individual score in a World Cup match. Playing against the United Arab Emirates at Rawalpindi in 1996, Kirsten scored 188 not out. Kirsten was also a bowler, well-known for his off-break style.

## GREATEST NUMBER OF SIXES IN A WORLD CUP MATCH

India's former captain, Sourav Ganguly, has a record 23 sixes to his credit from 18 World Cup matches. He broke the previous record of Viv Richards of the West Indies, who scored 22 in his career. Ganguly also holds the record partnership of 318 runs with Rahul Dravid for the second wicket in the 1999 World Cup.

## HIGHEST RUN SCORER IN WORLD CUP

The Indian cricketer Sachin Tendulkar is the highest run scorer in World Cup cricket. With an amazing strike rate of 88.91, he has scored 2,278 runs in the World Cup matches. Following him in the scoring league is Ricky Ponting of Australia who has scored 1,743 runs and has a strike rate of 79.95.

## MOST FIFA WORLD CUP WINS

Brazil has won the FIFA World Cup more times than any other team. In the competition's history, Brazil has won the title five times. Italy is a close second with four wins. Germany has won three times. Uruguay and Argentina have bagged the title two times each. Both England and France have been able to kiss the gold cup once. Hungary and Holland have reached the finals two times each.

## HIGHEST NUMBER OF SPECTATORS AT A MATCH

The most spectators to watch a single World Cup match was 174,000, for the 1950 World Cup final between Brazil and Uruguay, at the Maracana stadium in Rio de Janeiro, Brazil! On March 9, 1977, 162,764 people thronged to see the World Cup qualifier match between Brazil and Colombia. The third largest crowd goes to the Stadium of Light in Lisbon, Portugal, where a FIFA World Youth Championship match between Portugal and Brazil on June 30, 1991, was watched by 127,000 spectators. Modern 'all-seater' regulations and safety measures make these crowd sizes impossible today.

## MOST WORLD CUP HAT-TRICKS

Sandor Kocsis, Just Fontaine, Gerd Mueller and Gabriel Batistuta: all four players hold the record for the highest number of hat-tricks scored in the World Cup. Sander Kocsis of Hungary was the first to score two hat-tricks in any World Cup tournament — one against Korea, the other against Germany, both in 1954. Just Fontaine, of France, scored his double hat-trick in 1958. Gerd Mueller, the German striker, scored two hat-tricks at the 1970 World Cup. Argentina's Gabriel Batistuta (right) joined the double hat-trick scorers' club in 1998.

## HIGHEST GOALSCORER IN A SINGLE WORLD CUP

Just Fontaine of France scored 13 goals in the 1958 World Cup - a record that still stands! The Hungarian Sandor Kocsis is a close second, having scored 11 goals in the 1954 World Cup. Gerd Mueller of Germany scored 10 goals in the 1970 World Cup, placing him third.

## YOUNGEST PLAYER TO APPEAR IN THE WORLD CUP FINALS

Norman Whiteside of Northern Ireland became the youngest player to appear in the World Cup finals in 1982: he was 17 years and 41 days old. The Brazilian legend, Pele, previously held the record. He played in the 1958 World Cup when he was 17 years and 249 days old. Guiseppe Bergomi of Italy played the World Cup final in 1982 when he was 18 years and 201 days old. He stands third in the line-up of youngest players.

## BIGGEST WIN IN THE WORLD CUP

Hungary secured the biggest World Cup win in history when they beat El Salvador 10-1 in the 1982 tournament – breaking their own record of 1954 when they defeated Korea 9-0. Yugoslavia also registered a 9-0 win against Zaire in 1974. There have been three 8-0 wins: Sweden beat Cuba 8-0 in 1938, Uruguay beat Bolivia 8-0 in 1950 and Germany beat Saudi Arabia 8-0 in 2002.

## MOST GOALS IN A WORLD CUP CAMPAIGN

Hungary scored 27 goals in the 1954 World Cup tournament — the highest so far. In the same year Germany scored 25 goals, placing them a close second. France is third with 23 goals in the 1958 World Cup tournament.

### Did You Know?

When Juan Jose Tramutola coached Argentina during the first World Cup tournament in 1930, he was just 27 years and 267 days old. He still remains the youngest coach. The oldest coach ever was Cesare Maldini of Italy. He was 70 years, 131 days old at the 2002 tournament.

## MOST WORLD CUP TOURNAMENTS AS A COACH

Carlos Alberto Parreira of Brazil and Bora Milutinovic of Yugoslavia have coached World Cup teams five times in their careers. Walter Winterbottom of England, Sepp Herberger and Helmut Schoen of Germany, Lajos Baroti of Hungary and Henri Michel have all coached a team in the World Cup finals four times.

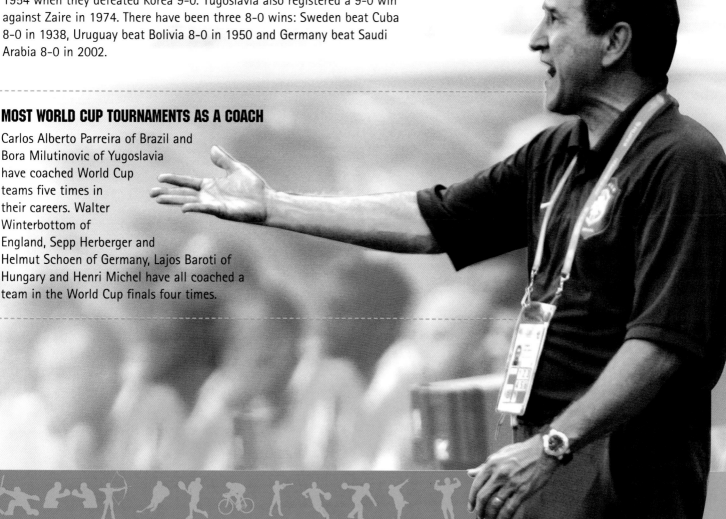

## FASTEST PITCH

Aroldis Chapman holds the record for the fastest recorded pitch speed in Major League Baseball history, after throwing a 105.1 mph (169.1 km/h) fastball in 2010. This beats the record of 100.9 mph (162 km/h) previously held by Lynn Nolan Ryan, which he set in 1974.

## MOST PITCHES

Denton True 'Cy' Young, known to be one of the greatest pitchers in baseball, retired with a record 511 victories – 94 more than second-place, Walter Johnson. Young pitched for five different major league teams from 1890 to 1911. Young still holds the records for the most career innings pitched (7,355) and the most career games started (815). Young also has an award named after him which is given to the pitcher voted the most effective in each of the two leagues.

## LONGEST BASEBALL THROW

Glen Gorbous, a Canadian baseball player, holds the record for the world's longest baseball throw. While playing for Omaha in the American Association, Gorbous threw the ball 135.89 m (445.8 ft). The throw beat the previous record held by Don Grate by a whole 22.86 cm (9 in), that was set in Minneapolis on August 27, 1956.

## MOST HOME RUNS IN A CAREER

Barry Lamar Bonds, left fielder for the San Francisco Giants, is considered the home run king of baseball. With 762 home runs, he surpassed Hank Aaron's career best of 755 to set a new record. Not only is he the leading home run scorer, he also has to his credit the highest number of Most Valuable Player awards, with seven. He also holds several other records, including the most number of walks (2,553) and the most home runs in a single season (73).

**Did You Know?**

Joe Morgan was the first player in the history of baseball to steal 500 bases and hit 200 home runs in the year 1978.

## MOST WORLD SERIES HOME RUNS

Mickey Mantle, an American baseball player, holds many records, including the most World Series home runs, with 18 in total. He also made 40 RBIs, 42 runs, 43 walks, 26 extra-base hits, and 123 total bases. He was elected to the Baseball Hall of Fame in 1974, along with his former teammate Whitey Ford. Mantle is credited with the longest measured home run in a Major League Game, at 193 m (633 ft). The record was set in a game for the New York Yankees against the Detroit Tigers in 1960.

## YOUNGEST PLAYER TO HIT 500 HOME RUNS

Alex Rodriguez, of the Yankees, became the youngest player to hit 500 career home runs. Rodriguez also won the Most Valuable Player award in 2005. He surpassed Jimmie Foxx as the youngest player to reach 500 homers. Rodriguez's 500th came in his 1,855th game. Besides Rodriguez, only two players took fewer games to reach the 500 mark — Mark McGwire in 1,639 games and Babe Ruth in 1,740 games. In 2007 Rodriguez signed a $275 million contract with the New York Yankees becoming the highest salaried player!

## MOST SUCCESSFUL COACH

Phil Jackson, former coach of the Los Angeles Lakers, is considered to be one of the best coaches in the history of the National Basketball Association. He currently holds the record for the most number of play-off game wins as a coach and has also won 9 NBA titles as a coach, a record shared with Red Auerbach.

### HIGHEST NUMBER OF CONSECUTIVE FREE THROWS

The record for the highest number of consecutive free throws is held by Ted St. Martin. Martin, a professional basketball free throw shooter, sank 5,221 consecutive free throws in Florida in 1996!

### GREATEST NUMBER OF THREE-POINT FIELD GOALS

The record for the most three-point field goals in NBA history is held by Ray Allen. Allen currently plays for the Miami Heat and has also played for the Milwaukee Bucks, Seattle SuperSonics, and Boston Celtics. He has scored 2,912 three-pointers to date.

### Did You Know?

Getting balls out of the basket was quite a tedious task in earlier days: ladders had to be used because the baskets were closed at the bottom!

## HIGHEST NUMBER OF POINTS IN A SINGLE GAME

Wilton Norman Chamberlain is the only basketball player to average more than 50 points a game for a whole season and also has to his credit the NBA single-game record for the highest number of points. In 1962, in a 169-147 Warriors victory over the New York Knicks in Pennsylvania, he scored 100 points to become the first and only NBA player to ever do so. For his various accomplishments, he was inducted into the Basketball Hall of Fame in 1978.

## FIRST ROOKIE TO WIN THE SIXTH MAN AWARD

Ben Gordon, an American National Basketball Association player for the Chicago Bulls, was the first rookie in the history of the NBA to win the Sixth Man Award. The award is given to the league's best substitute, or sixth man. He averaged 15.1 points, 2.6 rebounds, and 1.9 assists per game in the 2004–05 season.

## MOST POINTS, REBOUNDS AND MVPS

Kareem Abdul-Jabbar, a retired American professional basketball player and current assistant coach, holds the record for the most number of points (38,387) scored in basketball. He also won a record six Most Valuable Player Awards. Jabber played on six championship teams as a professional, and also played on three NCAA championship teams. In 1975 he recorded 1,111 defensive rebounds in his first season with the LA Lakers. This remains the NBA single-season record.

## MOST CAREER BLOCKS

Hakeem Olajuwon, a retired Nigerian-American professional basketball player holds the NBA record for the most blocks in a career – a staggering 3,830! In the 1993-94 season, this great player also became the only player in NBA history to win the NBA's Most Valuable Player, Defensive Player of the Year and Finals MVP awards in the same season. He is also known for his great footwork. His set of fakes and spin moves became known as his trademark 'Dream Shake'! For his outstanding career, Olajuwon was selected as one of the 50 greatest players in NBA history.

### HIGHEST POINTS SCORER IN RUGBY WORLD CUP HISTORY

England's Jonny Wilkinson holds the Rugby World Cup points record with 277 and is the only player to score points in two Rugby World Cup Finals. The previous record holder was Scotland's Gavin Hastings with 227 points.

### COUNTRY SHOWN THE MOST RED CARDS IN A WORLD CUP

The record for the most players shown the red card during a World Cup is held jointly by Tonga and Canada, with a total of three each, just a little ahead of Samoa, South Africa and Wales, who each have two.

### MOST POINTS AND WIDEST WINNING MARGIN IN A WORLD CUP GAME

The highest number of points scored in a single World Cup game is 145 – by New Zealand against Japan in 1995. The widest points margin between teams is 142, from a game where Australia beat Namibia in 2003.

## COUNTRY WITH THE GREATEST NUMBER OF APPEARANCES IN A WORLD CUP

The New Zealand All Blacks and France have both played the greatest number of matches in the Rugby Union World Cup, each playing 43 matches in the tournament's short history. The next in line is Australia with 41 matches and then England, who have appeared 40 times in the tournament.

## TOP TRY-SCORER IN THE WORLD CUP

New Zealand's Jonah Lomu is the top try-scorer in the history of the World Cup, with 15 tries to his name. A powerhouse of New Zealand rugby, Lomu made 11 appearances for them at the World Cup and is considered one of the best players of all time.

## THE MOST WORLD CUP APPEARANCES

Englishman Jason Leonard has played the most number of Rugby World Cup matches, making 23 appearances in his career. Second in line are Kiwis Sean Fitzpatrick and Richard Loe, along with the Englishman Martin Johnson with 18 appearances.

### Did You Know?

The record for the highest number of penalties converted in a World Cup is held by Gonzalo Quesada of Argentina, who kicked 31 in the 1999 tournament.

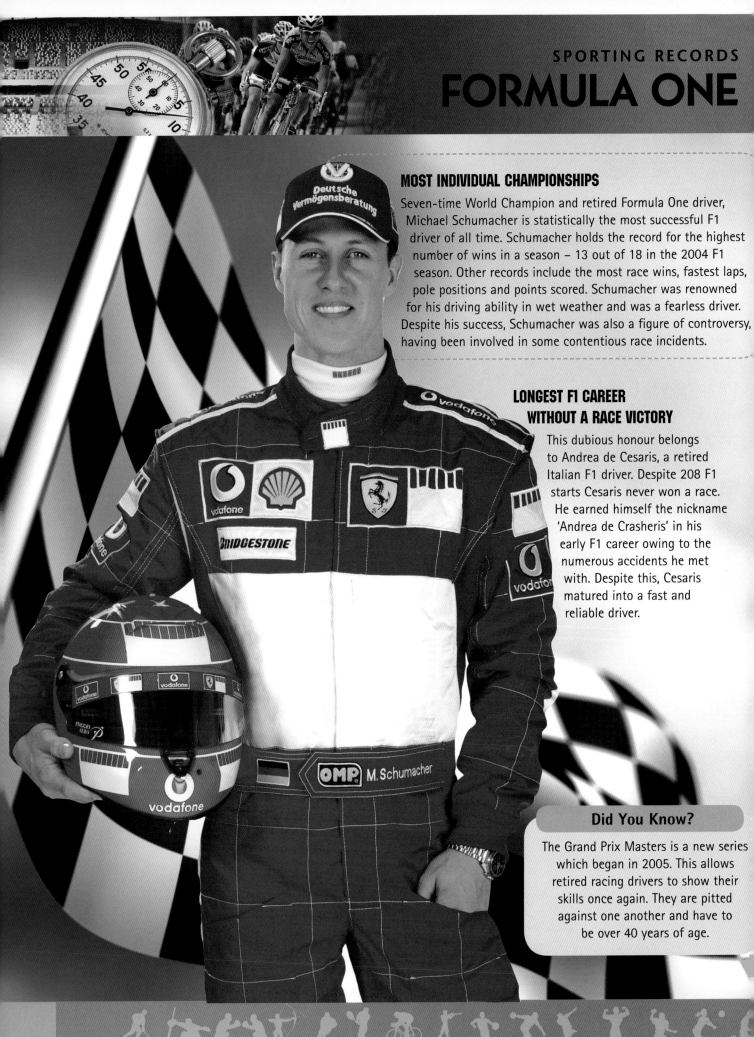

## MOST INDIVIDUAL CHAMPIONSHIPS

Seven-time World Champion and retired Formula One driver, Michael Schumacher is statistically the most successful F1 driver of all time. Schumacher holds the record for the highest number of wins in a season – 13 out of 18 in the 2004 F1 season. Other records include the most race wins, fastest laps, pole positions and points scored. Schumacher was renowned for his driving ability in wet weather and was a fearless driver. Despite his success, Schumacher was also a figure of controversy, having been involved in some contentious race incidents.

## LONGEST F1 CAREER
## WITHOUT A RACE VICTORY

This dubious honour belongs to Andrea de Cesaris, a retired Italian F1 driver. Despite 208 F1 starts Cesaris never won a race. He earned himself the nickname 'Andrea de Crasheris' in his early F1 career owing to the numerous accidents he met with. Despite this, Cesaris matured into a fast and reliable driver.

### Did You Know?

The Grand Prix Masters is a new series which began in 2005. This allows retired racing drivers to show their skills once again. They are pitted against one another and have to be over 40 years of age.

## MANUFACTURER WITH MOST GRAND PRIX WINS

Ferrari, with its base in Maranello, Italy, holds the record for the manufacturer with the most number of Grand Prix wins. With 221 wins from 1961 to the end of the 2013 F1 season and associations with world class racing drivers like Michael Schumacher and Rubens Barrichello, Ferrari has recorded unparalleled success. They also have the distinction of holding many of the most prestigious records, including most constructors' championships, most wins in a season, most drivers championships and more.

## ONLY RACING DRIVER TO HOLD F1 AND
## INDY CAR TITLES AT THE SAME TIME

Nigel Mansell, the most successful British racing driver, is the only person to hold both the F1 World Championship and IndyCar title at the same time. The 1992 season was his finest ever, when he started the year with five wins and recorded the highest number of pole positions (14), winning 9 races over the season. He also won the BBC Sports Personality of the Year twice, in 1986 and 1992 – one of only three people to do so.

Sebastian Vettel is the youngest ever F1 champion and one of the best racing drivers of this generation.

## MOST CONSECUTIVE WINS

The German racing driver Sebastian Vettel holds the record for consecutive wins, with 9 races won – he has won the Belgian, Italian, Singapore, Korean, Japanese, Indian, Abu Dhabi, United States and Brazilian Grand Prix during the 2013 season.

## YOUNGEST F1 CHAMPION

Sebastian Vettel is the youngest ever F1 champion – he won the championship in 2010 aged 23 years and 133 days, beating the previous record set by the UK's Lewis Hamilton by 168 days, which he had held since 2008.

## CITY WITH MOST NUMBER OF GRANDMASTERS

Beersheva in Israel has the highest percentage of chess grandmasters per capita than any other city in the world – a bizarre distinction indeed! In reality this equates to eight grandmasters, the majority of whom are immigrants from the former Soviet Union. The city is Israel's leading chess centre and the main club has to its credit many cups and national championships.

## SMALLEST HANDMADE CHESS SET

A goldsmith called M. Manikandan spent 10 days carefully making the smallest handmade chess set. The chess set he made was less than a quarter of the size of his palm. The chess board measured 24 sq/mm (0.94 sq/in) and the largest piece (the king) was 10 mm (0.39 in) high, while the smallest pieces (the pawns) measured just 5 mm (0.2 in) in height!

## LONGEST CHESS GAME

The longest tournament chess game ever played was between Ivan Nikolic and Goran Arsovic, with 269 moves. The game lasted for 20 hours and 15 minutes and ended in a draw! Held in Belgrade in 1989, this record is very unlikely to be broken due to new rules made in the game. According to these modifications a player can claim a draw if no capture has been made and no pawn has been moved for fifty consecutive moves.

## GREATEST NUMBER OF CONSECUTIVE AND SIMULTANEOUS GAMES PLAYED

Susan Polgar, a Hungarian-American chess player, set a number of records in 2005. She set the record for the most number of simultaneous games played (326 games), highest number of games won (309), most number of consecutive games played (1,131), and the highest percentage of wins (96.93 per cent). Polger also became the youngest published composer of a chess problem, at the age of four.

## LONGEST HOLDER OF THE WORLD CHESS CHAMPION TITLE

Born in 1868 at Berlinchen in Germany, Emanuel Lasker was a World Chess Champion, mathematician, and philosopher. He became the second World Chess Champion after his successful triumph over Steinitz, with ten wins, four draws and five losses. Lasker held the title for 26 years and 337 days — a feat unbeaten to this day!

### Did You Know?

Chess was banned in Iran after the 1979 Islamic Revolution. Leaders claimed that chess was a form of gambling and would cause harm to people and society. Ironically, chess is believed to have been born in Iran. The ban forced Iranian chess players to go underground. The ban was lifted in 1988 by Ayatollah Khomeini.

### MOST NUMBER OF CONSECUTIVE WINS

The Russian chess giant, Garry Kasparov, holds the record for the greatest number of consecutive wins (14) in professional tournaments. The earlier record for most consecutive wins was held by Anatoly Karpov. Kasparov has also received the 'Chess Oscar' – an international chess award given to the best chess player every year – a record eleven times! He is also renowned for defeating even the most powerful computers at chess.

### CONSECUTIVE TOUR DE FRANCE WINS

Spanish road racing cyclist Miguel Indurain won five consecutive Tours de France from 1991 to 1995, the fourth, and last, cyclist to win the race five times. He also won the Giro d'Italia twice, becoming one of only seven people in history to achieve the Giro-Tour double in the same season.

### MOST SUCCESSFUL TOUR DE FRANCE HILL CLIMBER

Richard Virenque is a retired French professional cyclist. He won the illustrious pink polka dot jersey, and title 'King of the Mountains', a record seven times at the Tour de France. The title is awarded to the best climber of the mountain section of the race. Virenque set the record in the 2004 season, breaking the previous best jointly held by Lucien van Impe and Bahamontes, who each won the jersey six times.

## GREATEST NUMBER OF COMPETITIVE VICTORIES

With a record 525 career victories, Eddy Merckx is considered the greatest cyclist of all time. Owing to his unquenchable thirst for victory, he earned the nickname 'The Cannibal'. His first win was recorded in the 1966 Milan-San Remo and he recorded his last major victory in the same place ten years later. Merckx is also the only cyclist to win all the classifications in a single season at the Tour de France and the Giro d'Italia.

### Did You Know?

The first cycling race on record was a 1,200 m (3,937 ft) race, held in 1868 at the Parc of Saint-Cloud, Paris. It was won by an expatriate Englishman, Dr. James Moore, who rode a bicycle with solid rubber tires. He also won the first cycling race between two cities.

## MOST NUMBER OF WORLD CUP RACE WINS IN A SINGLE SEASON

Paolo Bettini, a road cyclist from Italy, won the Milan-Sanremo, HEW Cyclassics and Clásica de San Sebastián in 2003, thereby setting the record for the most number of World Cup race wins in a single season. He also won the UCI Road World Cup series for three consecutive years in 2002, 2003 and 2004. Bettini belongs to the Belgian Quick Step-Innergetic professional cycling team and has been given the nickname 'Il Grillo', which means 'the cricket', because he is known to repeatedly attack, as well as for his style of cycling known as sprinting.

## OLDEST PROFESSIONAL CYCLIST

Fred Rompelberg is a Dutch cyclist best known for the ten World speed cycling Records he has set. Rompelberg became a pro-cyclist in 1971 and still has his licence, which makes him the world's oldest professional cyclist. He was also the Dutch Champion for the year 1977. In 1995, he set a World Record speed of 167.04 mph (268.831 km/h) for cycling, while being pulled by a dragster.

## FASTEST 500 METRE UNPACED FLYING START

Estonian Erika Salumäe holds the World Record for the 500 m (1,640.4 ft) unpaced flying start. She covered the distance in 29.6 seconds in the former USSR in 1987. Salumäe won as many as 10 gold medals, 3 silver medals and 3 bronze medals in world championships between the years 1981 and 1989.

## HIGHEST NUMBER OF PARIS-NICE RACE WINS

The former Irish road bicycle racer Sean James Kelly holds the record for the highest number of Paris-Nice race wins, recording seven consecutive victories between 1982-1988. Nicknamed 'the race to the sun', the Paris-Nice race is held each March and finishes on the Promenade des Anglais in Nice.

## HIGHEST NUMBER OF PGA PLAYER OF THE YEAR AWARDS

The highest number of PGA Player of the Year awards belong to Tiger Woods. He has won the title eleven times. Woods, an American golfer, ranks number one in his sport. He has won 14 professional major golf championships and 79 PGA Tour events. He has had more wins in his career than any other present golfer. Woods was also honoured with the title Associated Press Male Athlete of the Year four times.

## FIRST GOLFER TO WIN ALL FOUR MAJORS

American golfer, Jack William Nicklaus, who is generally considered to be the greatest golfer of all time, became the first golfer to win all four majors in a career. He won a record 18 professional majors in his PGA tour career which spanned 25 years. He also created a record by winning 8 majors on the Champions Tour. Both his records remain unbeaten to this day.

Legendary golfer and greatest Open Champion of all time, Harry Vardon had just one hole-in-one in his long career. This English golfer pioneered what became known as the 'Vardon Grip', a style of holding the club that is still popular among golfers today.

## YOUNGEST MALE GOLFER TO SCORE A HOLE-IN-ONE

Jack Paine holds the record of being the youngest male golfer to get a hole-in-one. In 2001 he scored a hole-in-one on the 66 yard 6th hole at Lake Forest Golf and Practice Course in California, aged just three years old.

## YOUNGEST FEMALE GOLFER TO SCORE A HOLE-IN-ONE

Rhiannon Linacare holds the record of being the youngest female golfer to score a hole-in-one. She scored the hole-in-one at 116 yard 17th hole at Coxmoor Golf Club at the age of nine and 75 days, beating the previous record holder, Katie Langley who was nine and 166 days old.

## LONGEST DRIVE

Karl Woodward, from the UK, was the first person in the history of golf to hit the ball 786.38 m (860 yards) in just two shots.

## MOST PLAYER OF THE YEAR AWARDS (WOMEN'S)

Annika Sörenstam from Sweden is one of the most successful female golfers in history. She has 69 official LPGA tournaments to her credit, including ten majors. Annika holds the record for winning the most number of Player of the Year awards (8) and she is the only female golfer to have shot a round of 59 in competition. She was the first woman to play in a men's PGA Tour event since 1945, and became the first player in LPGA history to finish a season with a sub-70 scoring average of 69.99. She also tops the LPGA's career money list with earnings of over $20 million.

### MOST NUMBER OF OLYMPIC GOLD MEDALS

India holds the most number of Olympic gold medals in hockey, winning 8 in total. Dhyan Chand, one of the greatest hockey players of all time, was part of the Gold-winning Indian team in three Olympic Games. India also holds the largest victory margin in an Olympic final by scoring 8 against Germany's 1 goal in 1936. India also holds the record for the most number of consecutive wins, with 30 victories on the trot from the year 1928 to 1960.

## LONGEST GAME PLAYED

In 2000 the National Hockey League All-Star game squad number 5 set the record for the longest game played. The team played for a record 18 hours, 55 minutes and 41 seconds during the Labatt Blue NHL pick-up marathon. The event was organised to raise money for the Hockey Fights Cancer charity.

## MOST GOALS

Pakistan's Sohail Abbas, a field hockey defender and penalty specialist, set the record for the most number of goals scored in an international competition. His record of 60 goals in 1999 beat the previous record of Netherlands' Paul Litjens (58 goals) and national record of Pakistan's Hassan Sardar (50 goals). Abbas also scored 274 international goals to surpass the previous record of Litjens that stood for 22 years.

## MOST SUCCESSFUL WOMEN'S TEAM IN THE WORLD CUP

Pakistan is the most successful women's hockey team in World Cup History. Pakistan has won the World Cup four times, with the Netherlands close behind on three times and Germany and Australia both having won it twice.

## MOST SUCCESSFUL MEN'S TEAM IN THE WORLD CUP

Pakistan is the most successful men's hockey team in the World Cup. They made six appearances and won four times in the years 1971, 1978, 1982 and 1994. The Netherlands are second in the list having made five appearances and won the title three times (1973, 1990 and 1998). Germany follows closely with two titles (2002 and 2006) to their credit.

## HOST WINNERS

Out of the nine nations that have hosted the Hockey World Cup, only the Netherlands and Germany have won the tournament as hosts. The Netherlands won in the years 1973 and 1998, while Germany won the title in 2006. Spain, England and Pakistan were host runners-up in the 1971, 1986 and 1990 tournaments. Australia came third when it hosted the tournament in 1994.

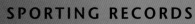

# TARGET SPORTS

## HIGHEST SCORE IN THE 72 ARROW MEN'S INDIVIDUAL RANKING ROUND

Im Dong-Hyun, a South Korean archer, set a World Record in the 72 arrow men's individual ranking round, with a score of 699 at the 2012 Summer Olympics. In 2006, Im competed in archery at the 2006 Asian Games and won two gold medals in the individual team events.

## WORLD RECORDS IN TRAP AND DOUBLE TRAP SHOOTING

Michael Diamond, a target shooter from Australia, holds the World Record in double trap shooting, as well as the final World Record in trap. It was in July 1998 that he won in the men's qualification round with 147 firings at Barcelona. He also holds the record for men's final in trap with 148 firings in 2007 at Nicosia. This skillful archer has two Olympic Golds and four gold medals in Commonwealth Games to his credit. Zhang Yafei of China holds the women's World Record in double trap with 115 firings in Nicosia in 2000.

## GREATEST NUMBER OF POCKET-BILLIARDS (POOL) CHAMPIONSHIPS

Ralph Greenleaf, a world famous American pool player, has the distinction of winning the most number of pocket-billiards championships. In his professional career, between 1919 and 1937, he won the world title championship as many as 19 times! Ralph started playing billiards at the young age of seven and became a city champion at twelve. At sixteen, he came fourth in his first world championship.

### Did You Know?

Neroli Fairhall of New Zealand was the first athlete in a wheelchair to compete at a regular Olympics in 1984. She was paralysed from the waist down in a motorcycling accident. Fairhall participated in shooting in the Olympic games.

## LONGEST TEN-PIN BOWLING MARATHON

The longest ten-pin bowling marathon lasted for 134 hr 57 minutes. Stephen Shanabrook at Plano Super Bowl in Plano, Texas set the record. Shanabrook completed a total of 643 games during his marathon. The record was previously held by Suresh Joachim who's marathon lasted for 100 hours.

## HIGHEST RUN IN 18.2 BALKINE BILLIARDS

One of the greatest all-round billiard players of all times was Willie Hoppe from the USA. He dominated the game of billiards for over twenty years and was nicknamed 'the king'. Hoppe set many records in the game that remain unbeaten. The most remarkable among these was a run of 622 in 18.2 balkine in the year 1912. He also set records in three cushion billiards.

## HIGHEST POINT SCORE IN MEN'S 10 METRE RUNNING TARGET COMPETITION

Manfred Kurzer of Germany set a World Record of 590 points in the men's 10 m running target competition at the 2004 Summer Olympics. The record was set at the Markópoulo Olympic Shooting Centre near Athens, Greece. Manfred scored the highest points in the qualifying round to beat the previous record of 588 points that was set by Igor Kolesov (May, 2002) and tied by Yang Ling (July, 2002).

## WORLD TITLES IN BOTH KARATE AND BOXING

The American Troy Glenn Dorsey is the only man to hold world titles in both karate and boxing. He began his career in karate. Soon after achieving his black belt he tried his hand as an amateur kick boxer. He later took this up as a profession, winning several titles sanctioned by KICK, ISKA and WAKO. He won a world title in kick boxing in 1987 and 1989 and the World IBF title in boxing in 1991. He also set the record for the highest number of punches thrown in a boxing match — 1,527 in a 12 round fight! He was voted the Fighter of the Year in 2002.

## YOUNGEST BOXING WORLD CHAMPION

Wilfred Benitez, a Puerto Rican boxer, has his name imprinted in the history of boxing for being the youngest ever World Champion. His speed, punching power and in-depth knowledge of the sport earned him the nicknames 'El Radar' and 'Bible of Boxing'. In 1976, at the age of just seventeen, he beat the twice World Champion, Antonio Cervantes, with a fifteen-round split decision. Benitez went on to become World Champion at three different weight divisions.

## LONGEST CAREER IN FENCING

Dr. Ivan Joseph Martin Osiier, a Danish fencer, who actually began his athletic career as an oarsman, holds the World Record for the longest career (40 years) in Olympics. He participated in seven Olympic games, but he won only one silver medal, in 1912. Osier has won 25 Danish National Championships in all the three fencing weapons — foil, epee and sabre. He is also one of the few athletes to have been honoured with the Olympic Diploma of Merit.

Al Couture, former welterweight champion, won the fastest knock-out in boxing history. He knocked down Ralph Walton in a little more than 10 seconds, on September 24, 1946.

## HEAVIEST WORLD CHAMPION IN BOXING

Nikolai Valuev holds the record as the heaviest and tallest boxer to become World Champion. At his prime the Russian boxer stood at 7' 11" and weighed in at 320lbs, he fought a total of 53 fights, winning 50 of them, with a total of 34 knockouts. Nikolai Valuev retired at the age of 36, following a majority-decision defeat to David Haye in November 2009.

## LONGEST REIGNING BOXING CHAMPION

Joseph Lois Barrow of Alabama, commonly known as 'The Brown Bomber', is the world's longest reigning boxing champion. He defeated boxing champion James J. Braddock on June 22, 1937, to lift the World Heavyweight Champion title. Barrow held on to his title for a record 11 years and 10 months until he finally retired on March 1, 1949. In his long career he knocked out 23 opponents in 27 title fights. He participated in 27 heavyweight championship fights – a record that stands to this day.

## MOST NUMBER OF WINS IN WRESTLING

Steve Austin holds the record for the most number of wins by an individual in the American World Wrestling Entertainment (WWE). He has a record six championships. Popularly known as 'Stone Cold', he made his debut in 1989. Austin has wrestled for several wrestling companies, including the World Championship Wrestling (WCW) and Extreme Championship Wrestling (ECW). He retired from the ring in 2003 due to neck, knee and ankle injuries and now makes his living as an actor.

## MOST GRAND SLAM SINGLES TITLES (WOMEN'S)

Margaret Smith of Australia, a former World Number 1 tennis player, won a record 24 Grand Slam singles titles. She won 62 Grand Slam titles in total – 24 singles, 19 women's doubles, and 19 mixed doubles – a feat that has not been matched since.

### MOST GRAND SLAM SINGLES TITLES (MEN'S)

Roger Federer, a Swiss tennis player, holds the record for winning the highest number of Grand Slam men's singles tournaments. He has won 17 titles. Just beating the previous record holder Pete Sampras, who won 14 titles. Roger is the only man to reach at least the semi finals of 23 consecutive Grand Slam Tournaments.

### MOST CAREER SINGLES TITLES (WOMEN'S)

Martina Navratilova, from the Czech Republic, is a former World Number 1 tennis player. Navratilova holds the record for the most number of singles titles in a career, winning an incredible 167 in her career. One of the greatest female tennis players of all time, she won a record 9 Wimbledon single's titles. Navratilova also holds the record for the longest unbeaten run in tennis history – 72 games in total.

### MOST CAREER SINGLES TITLES (MEN'S)

Jimmy Connors, a former American tennis player and World Number 1 for 160 consecutive weeks, won a record 109 men's singles titles in his career, including 8 Grand Slam singles victories.

## LONGEST SINGLES TENNIS MARATHON

The Austrian duo Hannes Hörndler and Patrick Fehringer hold the World Record for the longest singles tennis marathon ever played. They played for 26 hours and 5 minutes at the Tennisclub Allhartsberg, Austria, in September 2006.

## LONGEST DOUBLES TENNIS MARATHON

The longest doubles tennis marathon lasted 48 hours and 15 minutes! The doubles tennis match was played between Brian Jahrsdoerfer, Michel Lavoie, Peter Okpokpo and Warner Tse, all from the USA, at Houston, Texas, in April 2006.

### Did You Know?

Australian tennis player Samuel Groth has the fastest serve ever recorded in tennis. His fastest serve was recorded at 163.7 mph (263.4 km/h)

## MOST GRAND SLAM SINGLES IN A CALENDAR YEAR

Regarded as the best player of his generation, Roger Federer set a new record by winning three Grand Slam singles titles in a calendar year three times. He also made ten consecutive Grand Slam singles final appearances (a record) and is the longest ranking World Number 1, having taken the top spot on February 2, 2004. Federer has been named Laureus World Sportsman of the Year a record three years in a row.

# RACKET SPORTS

## MOST ALL ENGLAND OPEN CHAMPIONSHIPS (BADMINTON)

Sir George Alan Thomas won a total of 21 All England Open championships in his career. This phenomenal player from Britain won four singles titles along with nine doubles and eight mixed doubles titles. Apart from being a great badminton player, Sir George was also a good chess player and even appeared in the tennis doubles semi-finals at Wimbledon.

## FASTEST SMASH IN MEN'S DOUBLES (BADMINTON)

Fu Haifeng, a Chinese badminton player, set the record for the fastest smash in men's doubles. The smash speed was recorded at 206 mph (332 km/h) on June 3, 2004, at the Summer Olympics. He competed in the men's doubles along with his partner Cai Yun. His record-setting speed has made badminton the fastest racket sport in the world. He has won several other gold medals.

## MOST TABLE TENNIS WORLD CHAMPIONSHIPS

Hungarian table tennis player Viktor Barna won an incredible 40 World Championship medals — 22 gold, 8 silver and 10 bronze. In 1935, Barna won the singles, doubles and mixed doubles titles. His winning streak was cut short when he broke his playing arm in a car accident. He is still considered one of the best table tennis players to have ever lived. In the women's game, Angelica Adelstein-Rozeanu is considered the best table tennis player. Rozeanu started playing table tennis at the age of eight and by the time she turned 12 she had won her first tournament, the Romanian Cup. She won her first World Championship in 1950 and went on to win it for the next five years. Her record six successive World titles is yet to be matched.

## MOST OLYMPIC TITLES IN MEN'S TABLE TENNIS

Liu Guoliang of China holds the record for most Olympic titles in table tennis (male). He won both the singles and doubles (with Kong Linhui) in 1996. In his career Guoliang made a clean sweep of all the major titles. Guoliang started playing table tennis at the age of six, joining the national team in 1991.

## FASTEST SMASH IN SINGLES BADMINTON COMPETITION

The Indonesian badminton player, Taufik Hidayat, holds the record for the fastest smash in singles badminton competition, recorded at 189.5 mph (305 km/h). Hidayat has had an outstanding career, winning six Indonesian Opens, 2 Asian Games titles and 3 badminton Asia Championships. This master badminton player is also the current Olympic champion.

## MOST NUMBER OF WORLD TITLES (SQUASH)

Jahangir Khan of Pakistan, a former squash player, has his name securely listed in the record books for winning the most number of world titles. His record nine titles surpassed that of Jansher Khan from Pakistan, who was the previous record holder with eight title wins. Between the years 1981 and 1986, he won 555 matches consecutively! Jahangir is undoubtedly one of the greatest squash players to ever have played the game.

## HIGHEST NUMBER OF OLYMPIC TITLES IN TABLE TENNIS (WOMEN'S)

The highest number of Olympic titles in table tennis is shared between Chinese players Deng Yaping and Wang Nan. Both women have four Olympic titles to their names, both having won the women's doubles title twice. Deng Yaping has also won the women's singles title twice. Wang Nan has won the singles title once and the team title once.

### Did You Know?

The game of table tennis is also known as ping-pong, flim-flam, or even whiff-whaff. It was banned in the former Soviet Union for 20 years as it was believed to cause harm to the eyes.

### FASTEST 200 M AND 400 M SWIMMER (MEN'S)

Paul Biedermann, is a German swimmer from Halle, and a former 200 and 400 m freestyle long course world champion. He holds the long course and short course world records in 200 m freestyle, and the long course world record in the 400 m freestyle. His predecessor is Ian Thorpe, who previously held the world record for both of the these events. Thorpe has broken 22 world records and has to his credit 11 World Championship titles, 10 Commonwealth Games gold medals and nine Pan Pacific titles.

### FASTEST LONG COURSE FREESTYLE SWIMMING (MEN'S)

Cesar Cielo, a Brazilian professional swimmer is the World record holder for the long course men's 50 m freestyle swimming. He set a World Record in just 20.91 seconds. Cesar is the most successful Brazilian swimmer in history, having obtained three Olympic medals, winning six individual World Championship gold medals and breaking two World Records. He also holds the World Record for the long course 100m freestyle swim.

### FASTEST SWIMMER IN 400 M MEDLEY (MEN'S)

The American swimmer Michael Phelps holds many World Records, including the fastest time for the 400 m individual medley, which he set in 2002 and the men's 200 m butterfly which he set in 2001. Phelps' greatest achievement was the eight Olympic medals he won in Beijing in 2008, all of which were gold! Phelps currently holds 23 World Records and has been named World Swimmer of the Year four times!

## LONG DISTANCE SWIMMING

Lewis Gordon Pugh, a British swimmer, lawyer and environmentalist, known for his extraordinary capacity to withstand extremely cold temperatures, holds the record for the most southerly long distance swim. This great swimmer swam for 0.62 miles (1 km) at Petermann Island, off the Antarctic Peninsula. Last year he became the first person to swim the entire length of the Thames in order to spread awareness about the dangers of global warming. He is nicknamed the Polar Bear for his ability to swim in extremely cold water!

### 800 M FREESTYLE RECORD (WOMEN'S)

Katie Ledecky is an American distance swimmer, Olympic gold medalist, and World Record holder. Katie holds the current World Record in the 800 and 1500 m freestyle (long course). Her debut was at the 2012 Summer Olympics, when she was just 15-years old. Katie's success has earned her Swimming World's "World Swimmer of the year" and the American Swimmer of the Year award in 2013, as well as the FINA Swimmer of the Year award in 2013.

### GREATEST DISTANCE COVERED ON A JET SKI

Jeremy Burfoot, 51, from Torbay in Auckland holds the World Record for the greatest distance covered on a jet ski in 24 hours. Burfoot covered a distance of 2,287 km (1,421 miles) on Lake Karapiro, a man made lake on the Waikato River.

# WINTER SPORTS

## 5,000 AND 10,000 M SPEED SKATING (MEN'S)

The Dutchman Sven Kramer, the current reigning World Champion in long track speed skating, holds the World Records for the 5,000 m and 10,000 m distance. Born on April 23, 1986, Kramer is the son of former speed skater Yset Kramer. He set the record for the 5,000 m on March 3, 2007, in Calgary, Canada, at a recorded time of 6 minutes 7.48 seconds. The 10,000 m record was set on February 11, 2007, in Herenveen, at a time of 12 minutes 49.88 seconds.

## THE COUNTRY WITH THE MOST GOLD MEDALS AT THE WINTER OLYMPICS

Norway has won more gold medals at the Winter Olympics than any other country. It has to its credit 107 Winter Olympic gold medals and has won 303 Winter Olympic medals in total. Second in line is the United States with a total of 87 Olympic gold medals.

### Did You Know?

The Olympic Oval built in Canada for the 1988 Winter Olympics has been described as 'the fastest ice on Earth'. Its domed roof, high altitude and careful temperature control meant that World Records were set in no less than seven events during the course of the games!

## SKI JUMP WORLD RECORD (MEN'S)

Johan Evensen, a Norwegian ski jumper, holds the World Record for this unusual event. On February 11th 2011 he jumped 246.5 m (809 ft), in Vikersund, Norway. The following day he won his first world cup competition in the main event. Evensen announced his retirement from the sport just prior to the FIS Ski-Flying World Championships 2012.

## MOST NUMBER OF WORLD CUP SPRINT MEDALS

Germany holds the record for winning the most number of World Cup sprint medals in the 10,000 m event. Germany has won a record 20 medals in all – of which, eight are gold, eight are silver and four are bronze.

## OLDEST MAN TO WIN A WINTER OLYMPIC MEDAL

Anders Haugen was an American ski-jumper who competed in the 1924 Winter Olympics in Chamonix. He holds the record for being the oldest man to win a medal in the Winter Olympics. He received his bronze medal 50 years after he competed in the 1924 Winter Olympics after a scoring error was discovered in 1974!

## 5,000 M AND 10,000 M SPEED SKATING (WOMEN)

Martina Sáblíková, a Czech speed skater, won her first major tournament in 2007 during the European all-round championships in Collalbo. Sáblíková also won the 2007 Speed Skating World Cup at the 3,000 m and 5,000 m distance. On March 15, 2007, Sáblíková became the first female speed skater to skate 10,000 m in under 14 minutes when she set her record in 13 minutes and 48.33 seconds in Calgary – at the same time improving upon her own previous World Record by a full 20 seconds!

# GYMNASTICS

## MOST NUMBER OF OLYMPIC MEDALS

Larisa Latynina, a Russian gymnast, holds the record for winning 18 Olympic medals (9 gold, 5 silver and 4 bronze medals) between the years 1956 and 1964. No athlete in the history of the games has ever won so many medals. She was also the first woman at the Olympics to win nine gold medals. Larisa was an all-round champion in two Olympics and two World Championships.

## FIRST PERFECT 10 AWARDED IN A GYMNASTIC EVENT

Nadia Comaneci, a Romanian-American gymnast, was the first to be awarded a perfect 10 in a gymnastic event. Considered one of the finest gymnasts of all time, she has to her credit five Olympic gold medals. She was also honoured with the Olympic Order, the highest award given by the International Olympic Committee, in 1984 and 2004.

### Did You Know?

Edith Seymour of Great Britain holds the record for being the oldest gymnast to win a medal, securing a bronze medal at Amsterdam in 1928. She was 46 years old at the time.

## YOUNGEST GYMNAST TO WIN AN OLYMPIC MEDAL

Dimitrios Loundras, a Greek gymnast, was all of 10 years and 218 days when he won an Olympic bronze medal, making him the youngest medal winner in Olympic history. He participated in the parallel bars event at the 1896 Summer Olympics in Athens.

## COUNTRY WITH MOST NUMBER OF TITLES FOR RHYTHMIC GYMNASTICS

Bulgaria holds the World Record for the most rhythmic gymnastics team world titles. With a record nine team titles for the years 1969, 1971, 1981, 1983, 1985, 1987, 1989 (shared), 1993 and 1995, Bulgaria also boasts of highly successful and record-holding gymnasts like Maria Gigova, Maria Petrova, Simona Peycheva, Neshka Robeva and Yordan Yovtchev.

## MOST NUMBER OF INDIVIDUAL TITLES FOR ALL-AROUND RHYTHMIC GYMNASTICS

Born in 1975 in Bulgaria, Maria Petrova holds the record for the most individual world all-around rhythmic gymnastics titles, sharing the title with Bulgaria's Maria Gigova. Petrova began her career at the young age of five and was coached by Natalia Moravenova. She took second place in her first World Championship appearance in 1991.

## MOST NUMBER OF OLYMPIC MEDALS (MEN'S)

Male Gymnast Nikolay Andrianov, from Russia, holds the record for winning the most number of medals in the Olympic Games. He won 15 Olympic medals (seven gold, five silver and three bronze) between 1972 and 1980. His first international success was in 1971 at the European Championships in Madrid, where he won two gold medals.

**Ace:** A serve in racket sports that the opponent player fails to hit

**Athlete:** A sportsperson

**Balkline:** A line parallel to one end of a billiard table

**Base hit:** A hit that allows the batter to reach first base safely

**Black belt**: A black sash given to a person who excels in a martial art

**Block:** To deflect an opponent's shot in the game of basketball

**Extra base hit:** A hit that allows the batter to go past first base

**Free throw:** An unobstructed shot from the foul line awarded to a fouled player

**Hat-trick:** Three consecutive goals in a game, or a similar accomplishment, by the same sportsperson

**Hole-in-one:** When a player hits the ball directly from the tee into the hole with one shot

**Home run:** A hit by which the batter is able to make a complete circuit of the diamond and score a run

**Hurdles:** A race in which participants have to jump over a series of barriers

**Marathon:** A long distance running event of 26.21 miles (42.195 km)

**Penalty:** The punishment for breaking a rule during a game

**Pitch:** To throw the ball

**Red card:** A card that indicates that a player has been dismissed from a game

**Smash:** To hit a ball or shuttlecock in a forceful overhand stroke

**Sprint:** Short distance run

**Test cricket:** A five day cricket match in which each team plays two innings

**Triathlon:** An athletic event in which the participant has to swim, cycle and race over various distances

**Walks:** An advance to first base by a batter who receives four balls

**Yellow card:** A card shown to warn a player for violating the rules